Red and White Blood Cells! What, How and Why of Human Cells

Body Chemistry Edition

Children's Clinical Chemistry Books

pfiffikus

EDUCATIONAL BOOKS FOR CHILDREN K-12

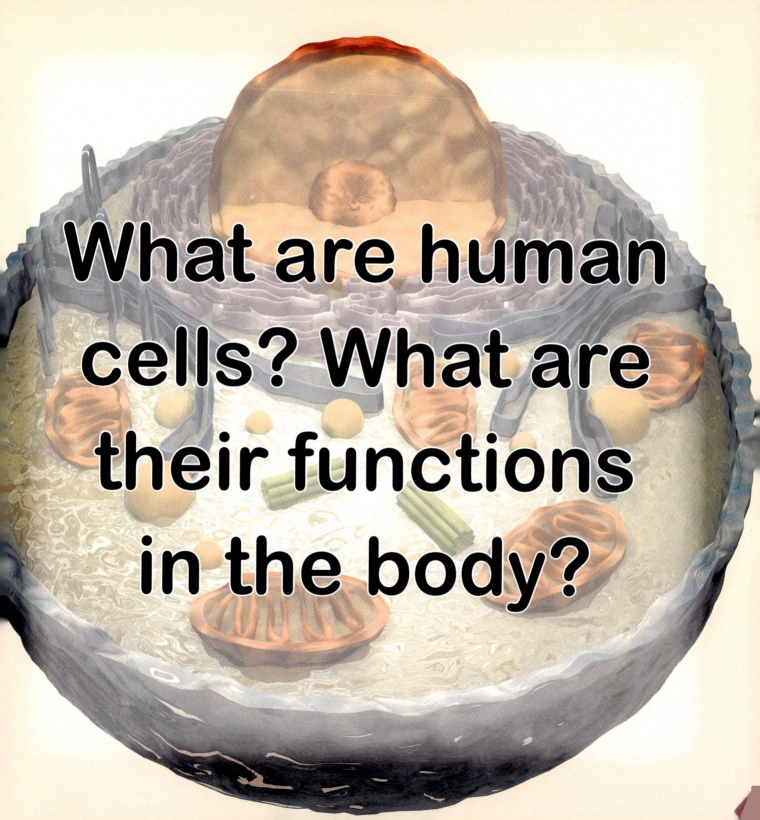

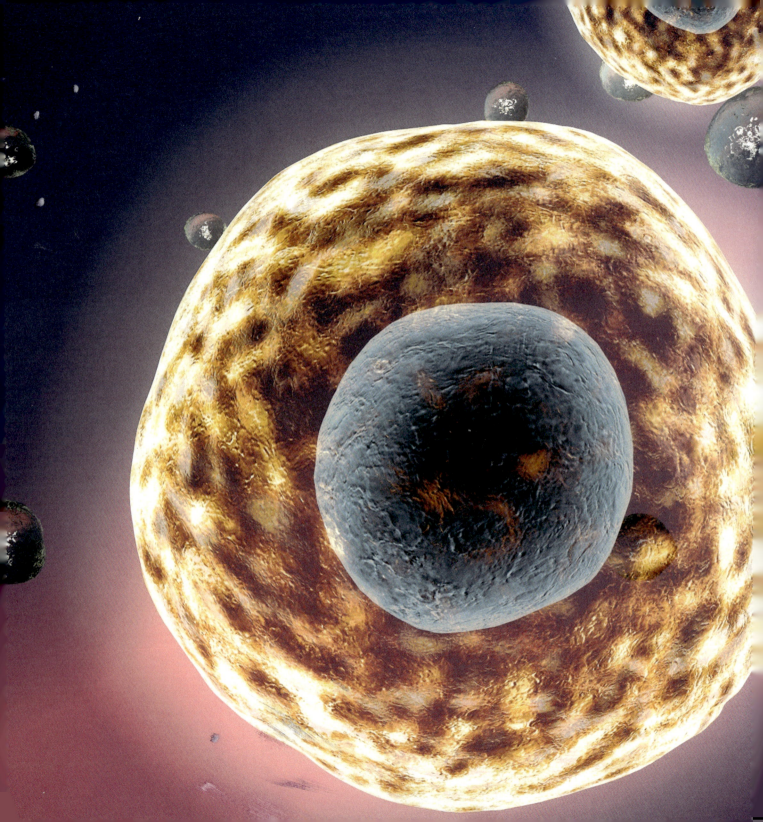

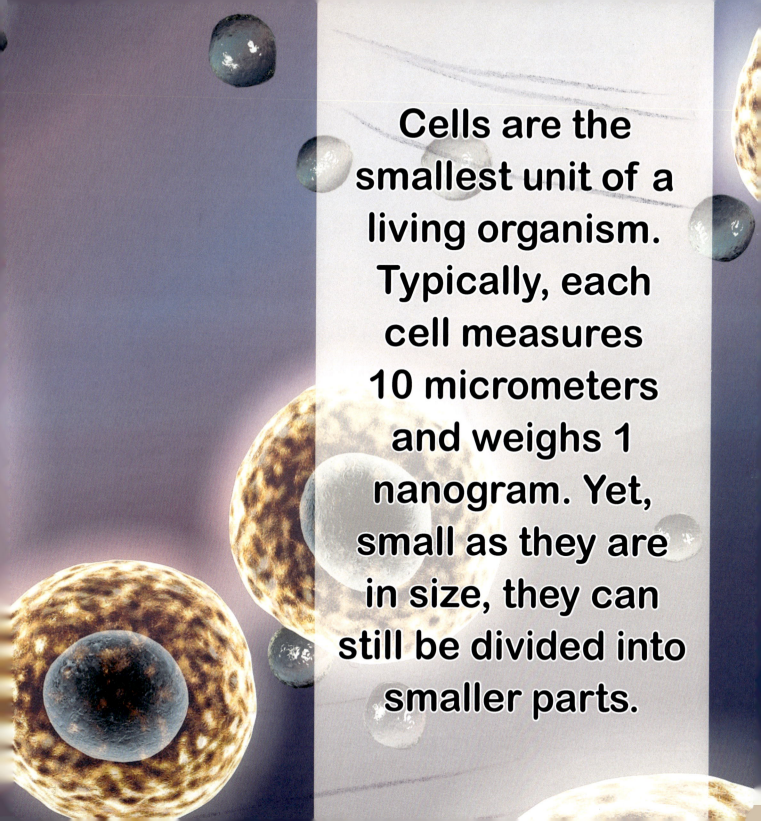

Cells are the smallest unit of a living organism. Typically, each cell measures 10 micrometers and weighs 1 nanogram. Yet, small as they are in size, they can still be divided into smaller parts.

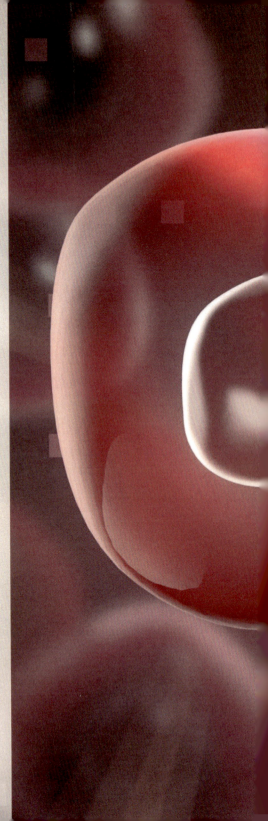

Each smaller part has its function. These cell parts or contents are held together by a membrane. The membrane has receptors. They react to the substances taken into the body as well as to the substances produced in the body.

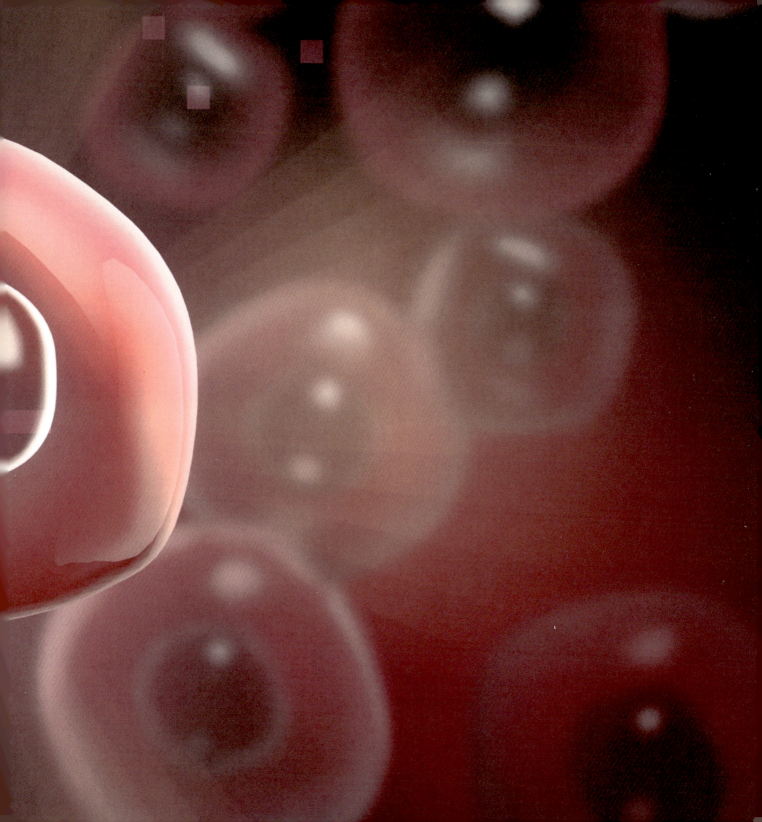

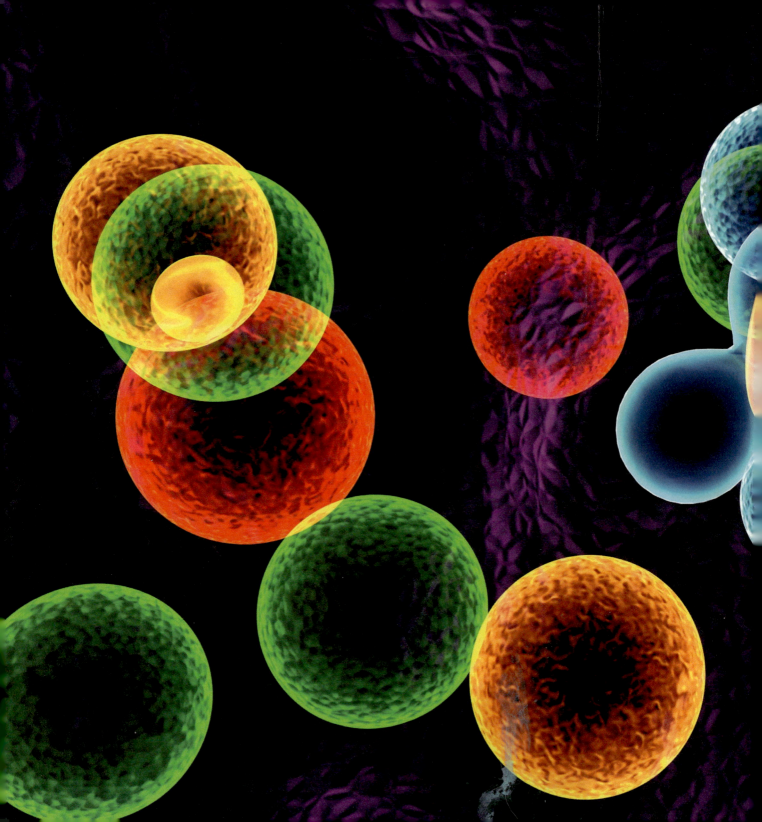

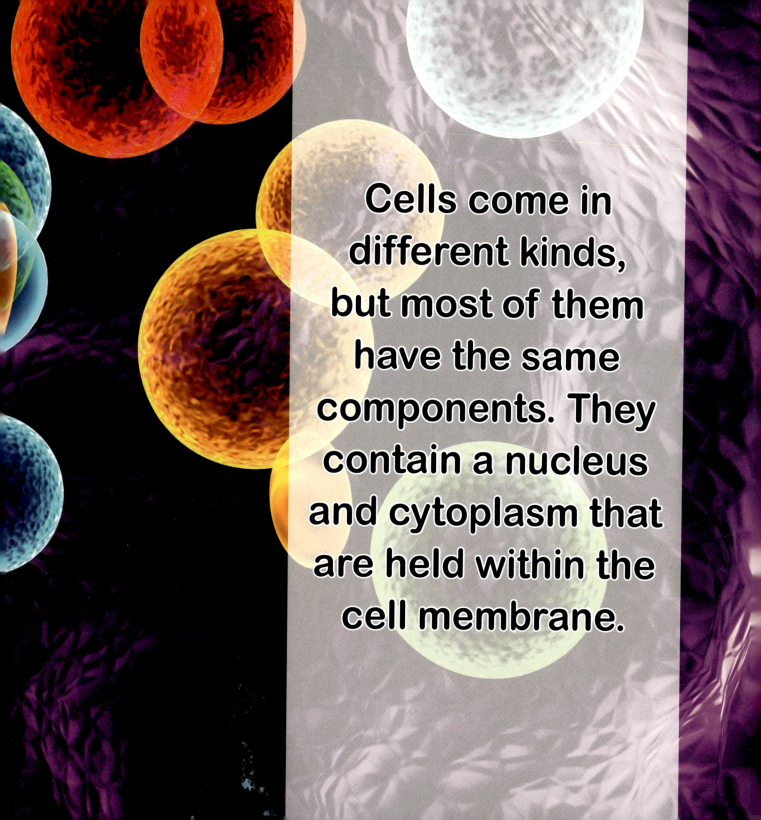

Cells come in different kinds, but most of them have the same components. They contain a nucleus and cytoplasm that are held within the cell membrane.

There are two compartments within the cell membrane. These are the cytoplasm and the nucleus. The structures that perform the cell's functions are found in the cytoplasm. Energy is also consumed and transformed here.

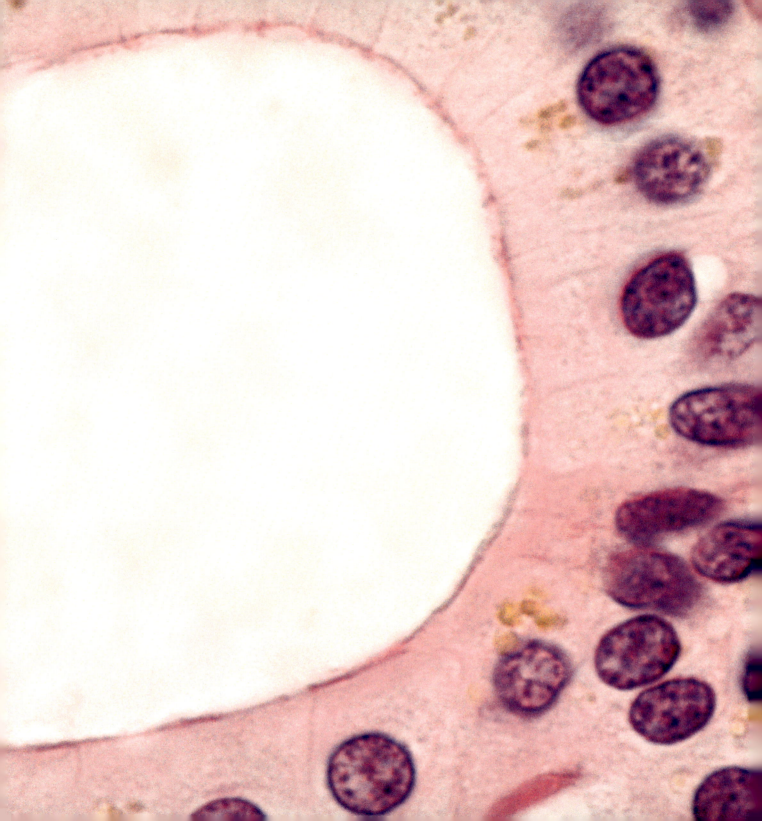

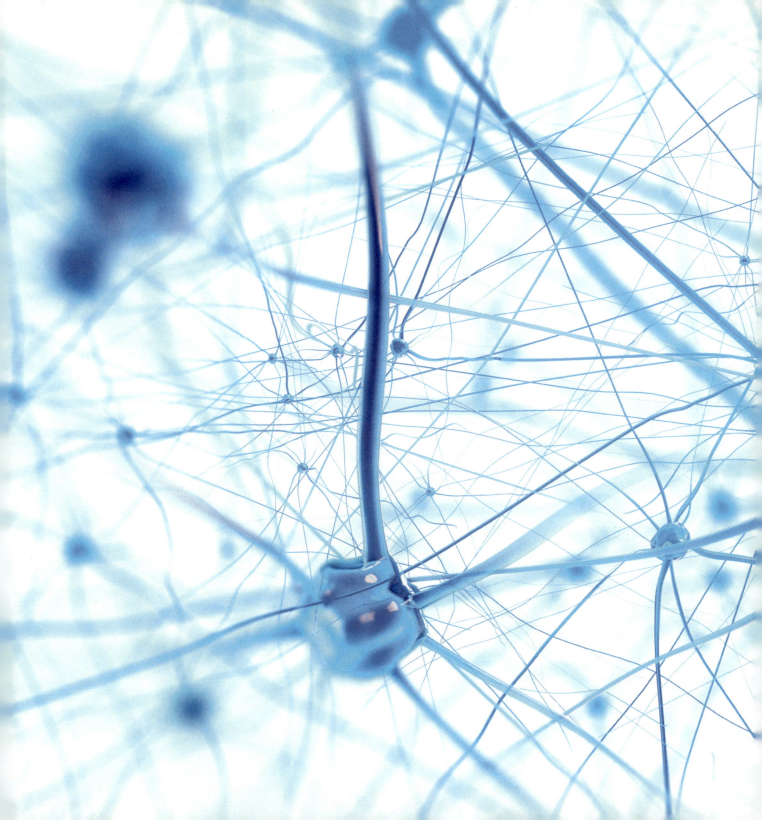

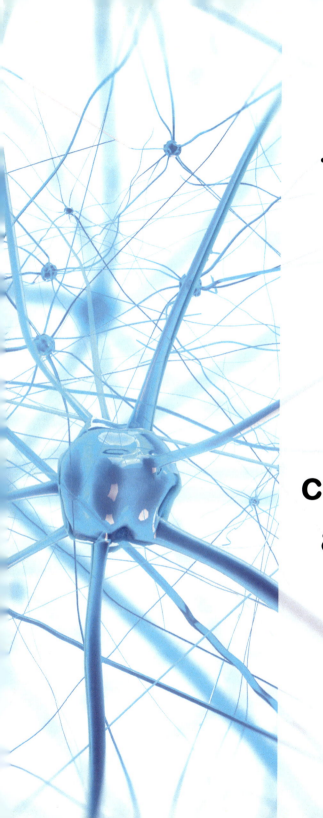

The cell's genetic material, the chromosomes, are housed in the nucleus. The structures that control cell division and reproduction are also found in this body.

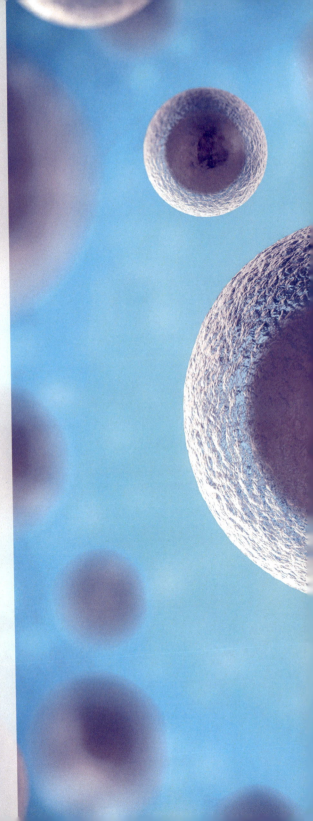

We already know that a cell is very small. But it is still composed of tiny structures that provide energy to the cell. These structures are called mitochondria.

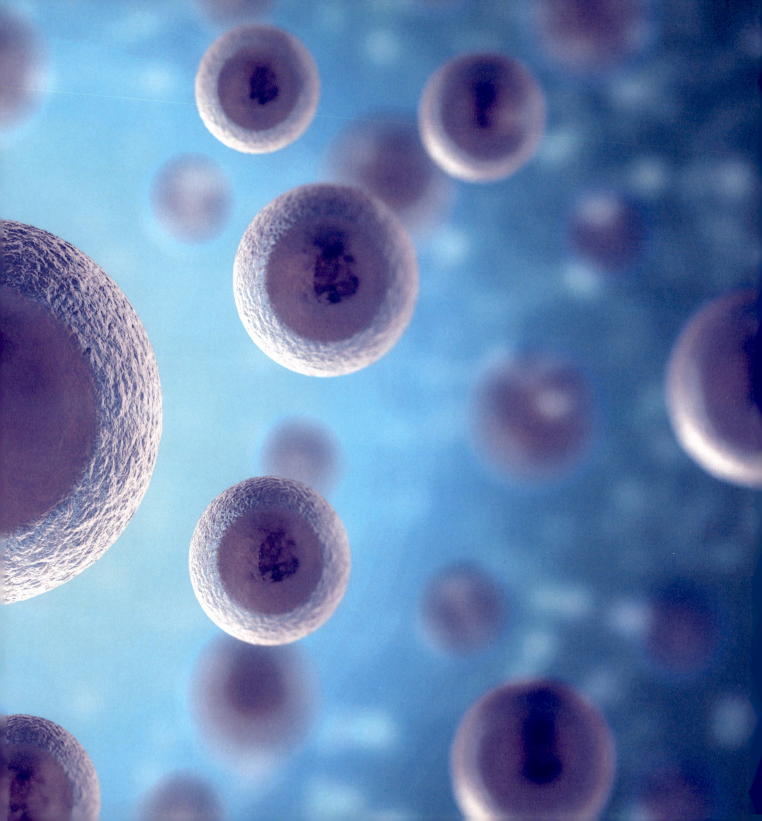

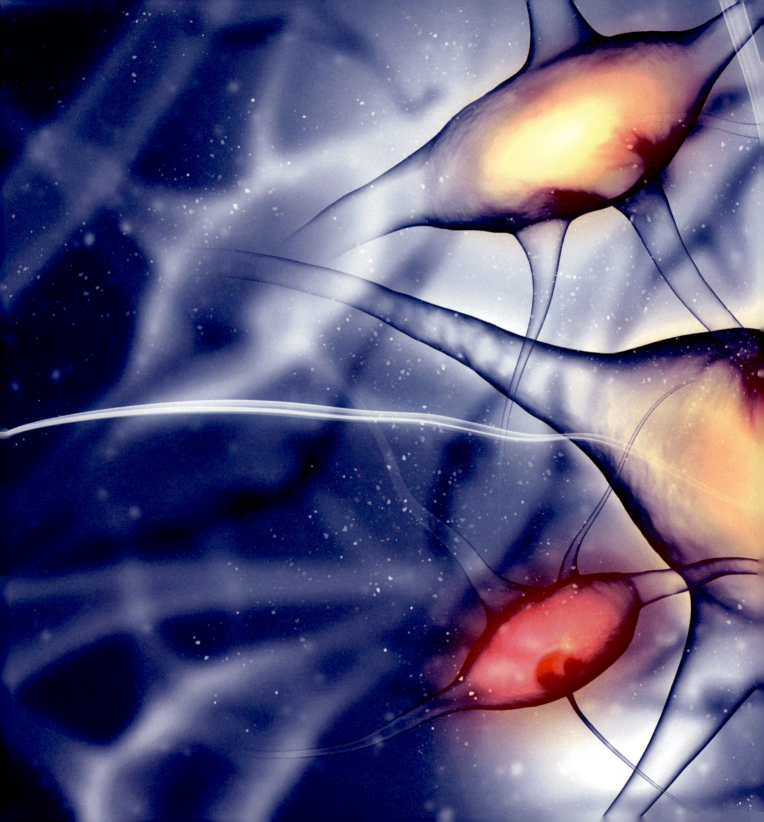

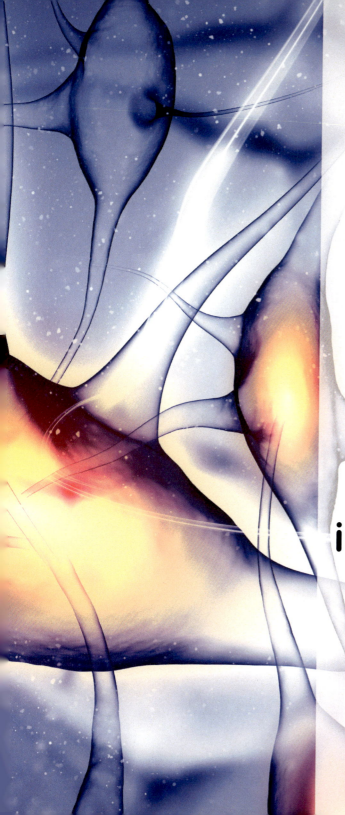

Our body has many different types of cells. Each of the cells has its own function and structure. The cell types include the blood, muscle, skin, bone, nerve and glandular cells.

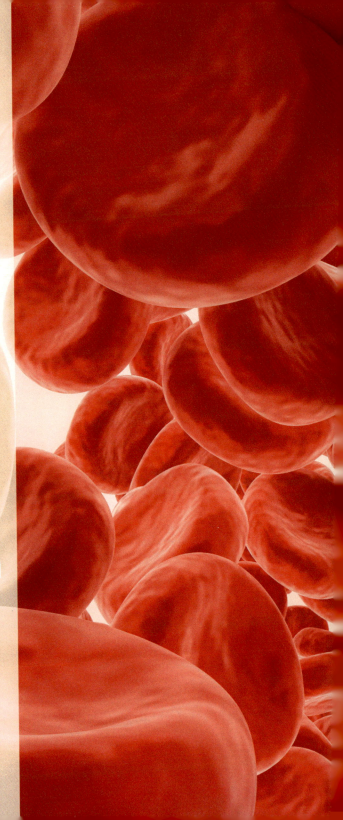

Blood cells are not attached to each other and move freely in the circulatory system. They float in the blood plasma. It is a yellow liquid which is 90% water, with various nutrients.

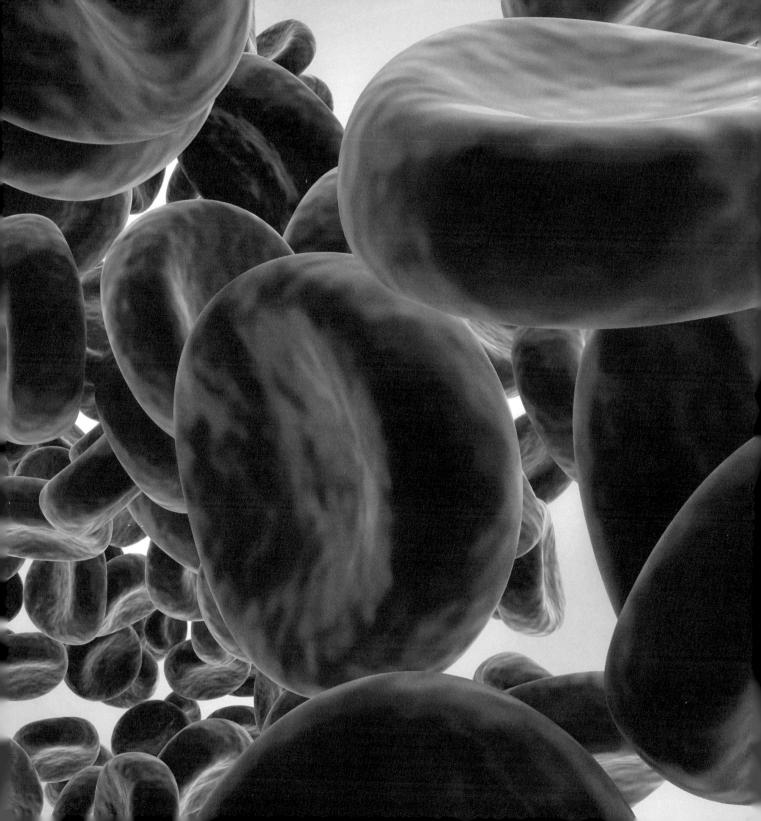

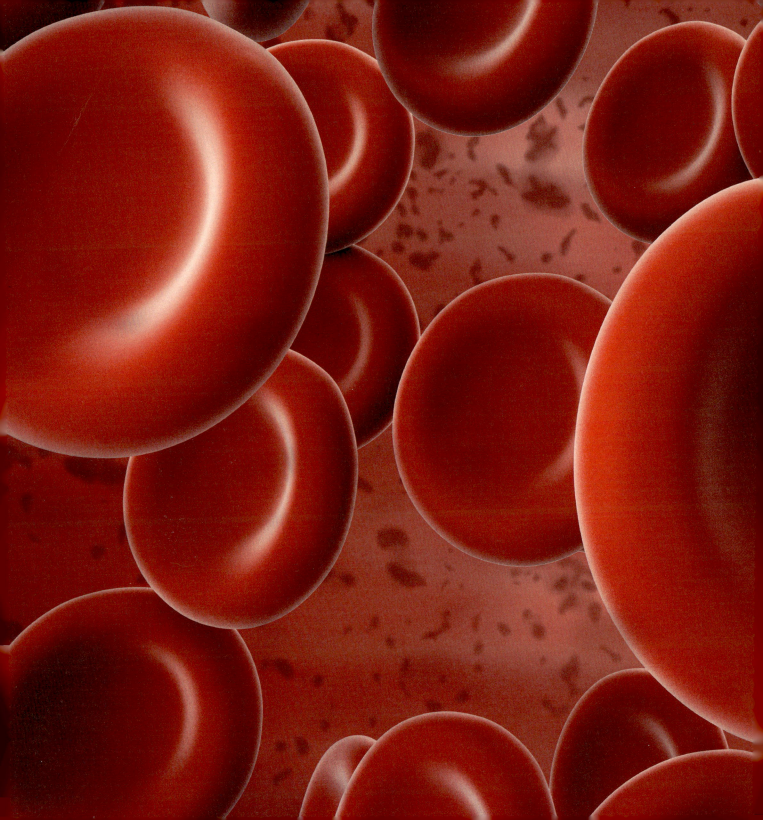

The red blood cells carry oxygen around the body. Its red color is due the presence of a protein called hemoglobin.

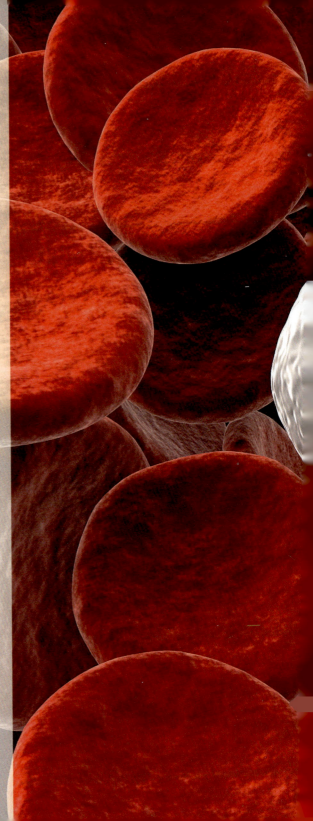

The white blood cells serve as the protector of the body from unwanted materials like bacteria, cancer cells, viruses and infectious diseases. They are an important part of the body's immune system.

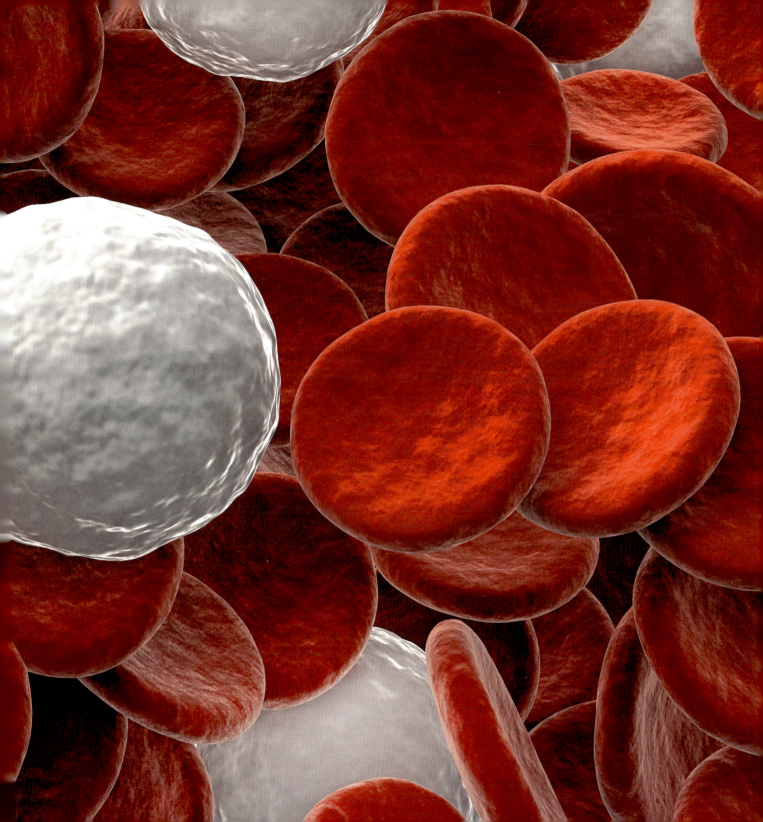

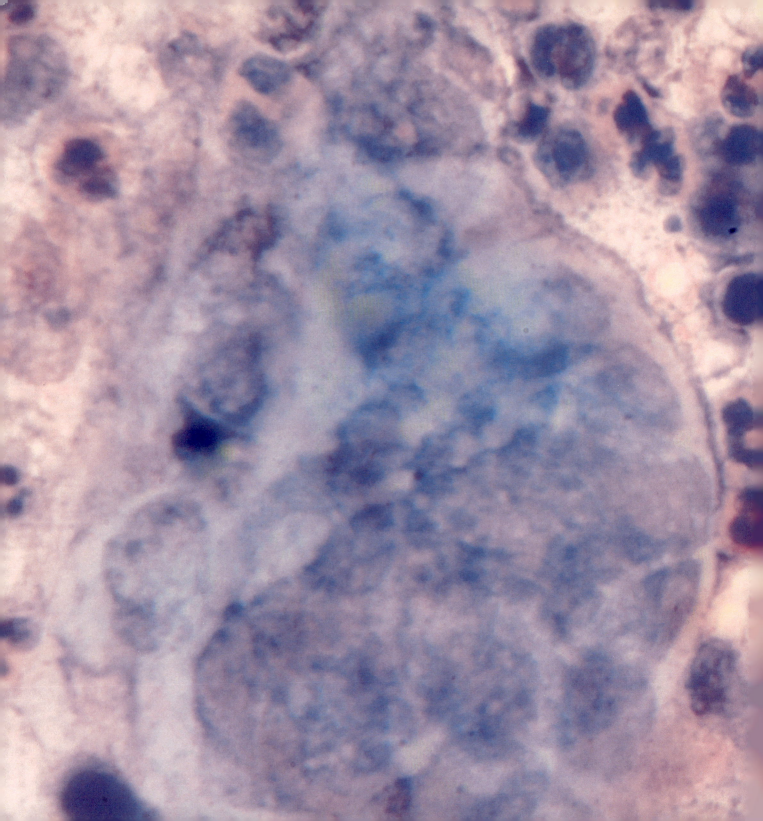

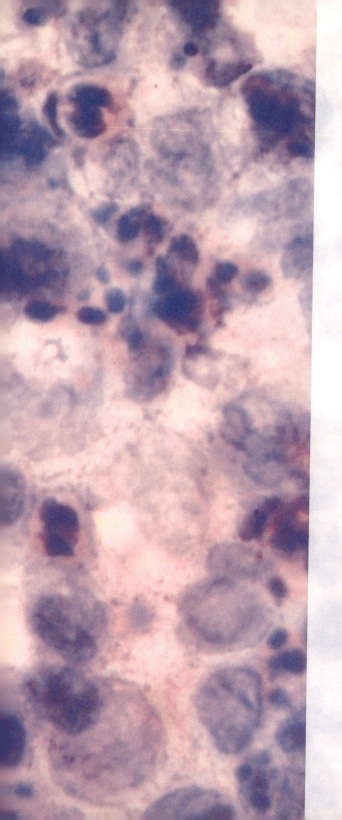

The muscle cells are the exact opposite, for they are firmly attached to one another. Muscles are soft tissues. They are for producing force and motion.

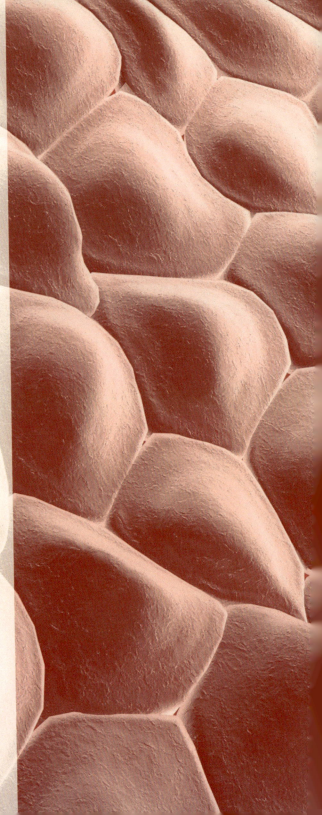

The skin cells can divide and reproduce quickly. The skin is considered as the largest organ of the body. The layers of the skin are the epidermis, dermis and the hypodermis, or subcutis.

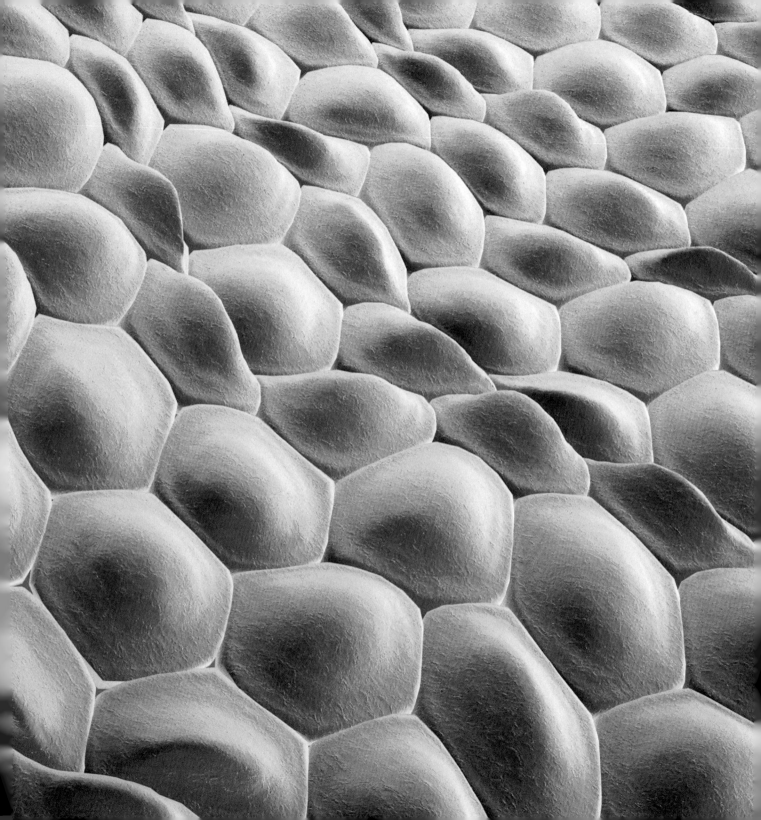

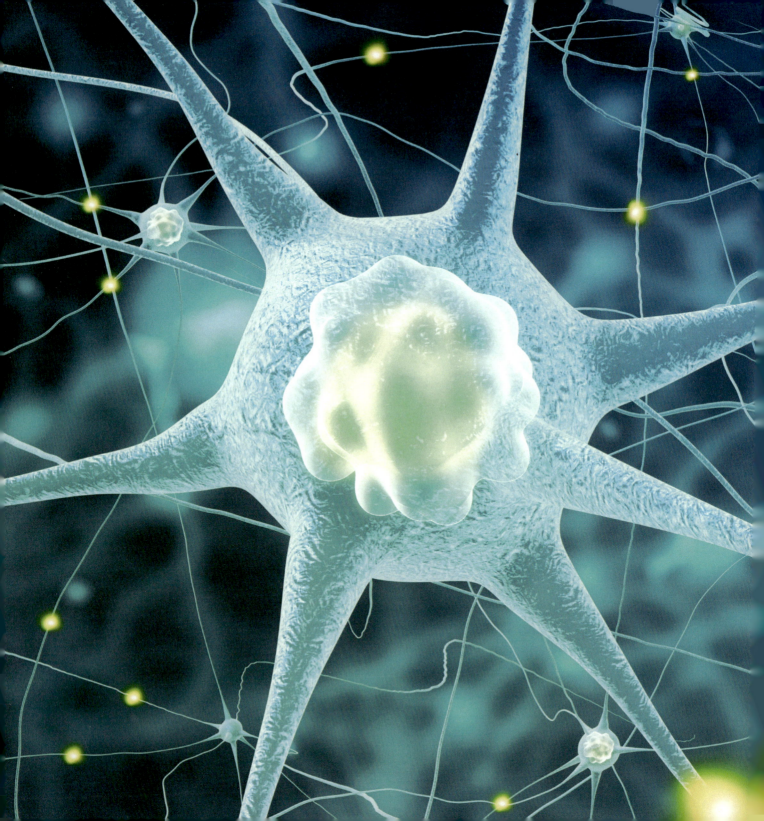

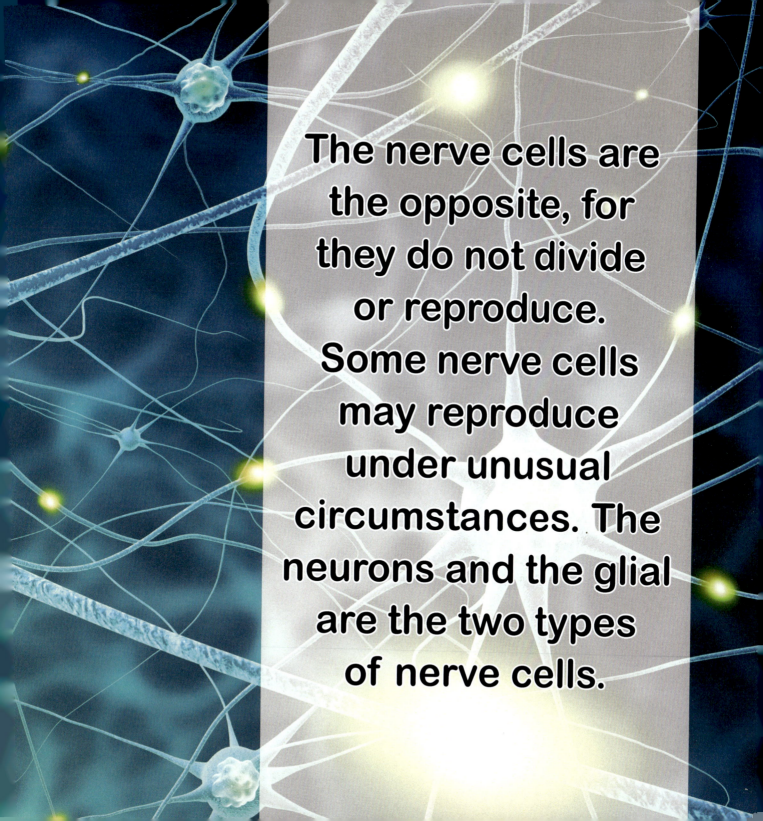

The nerve cells are the opposite, for they do not divide or reproduce. Some nerve cells may reproduce under unusual circumstances. The neurons and the glial are the two types of nerve cells.

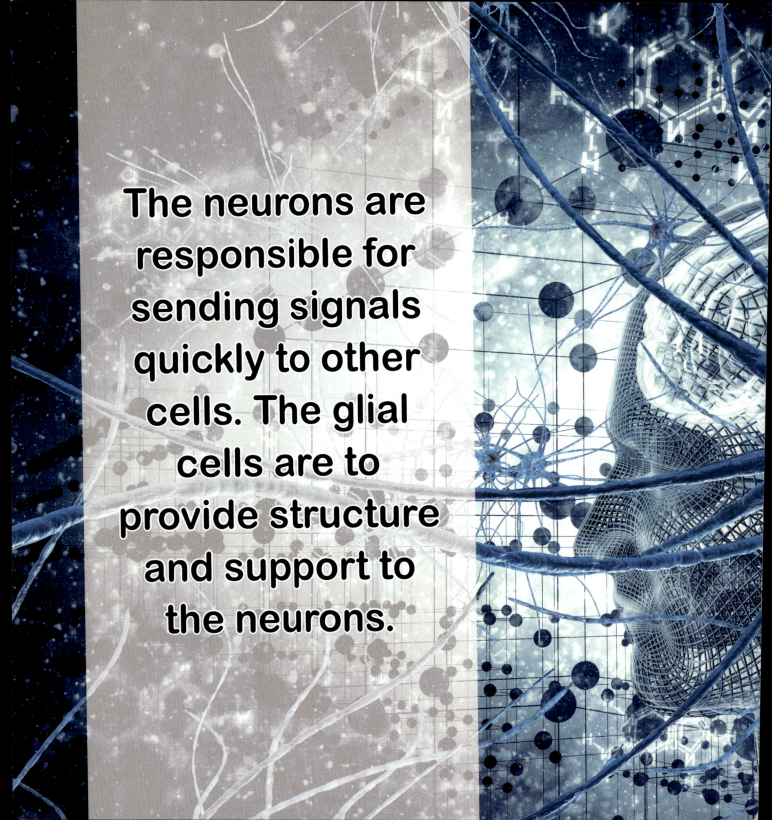

The neurons are responsible for sending signals quickly to other cells. The glial cells are to provide structure and support to the neurons.

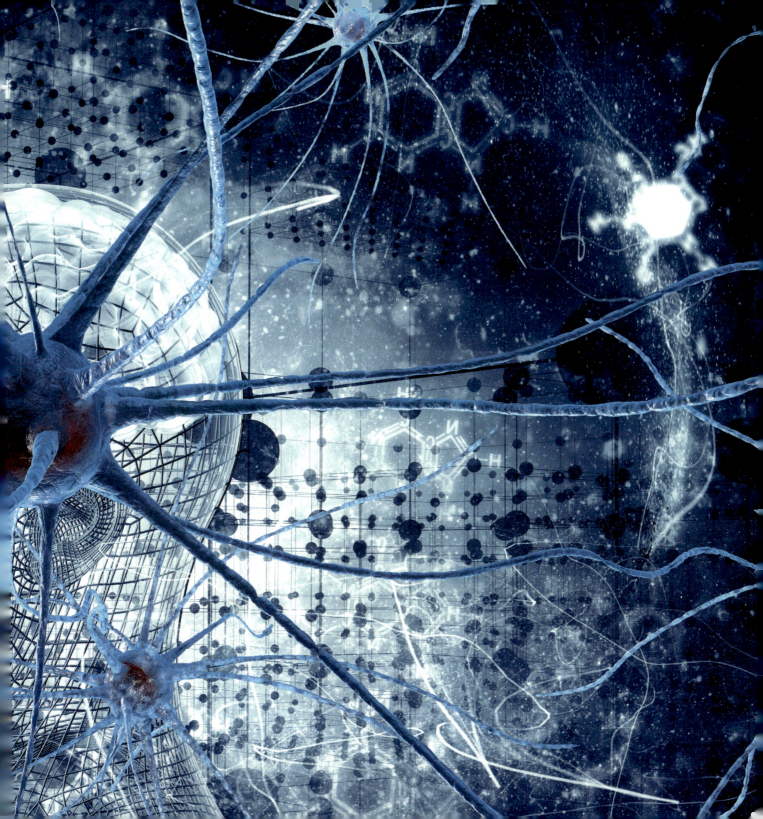

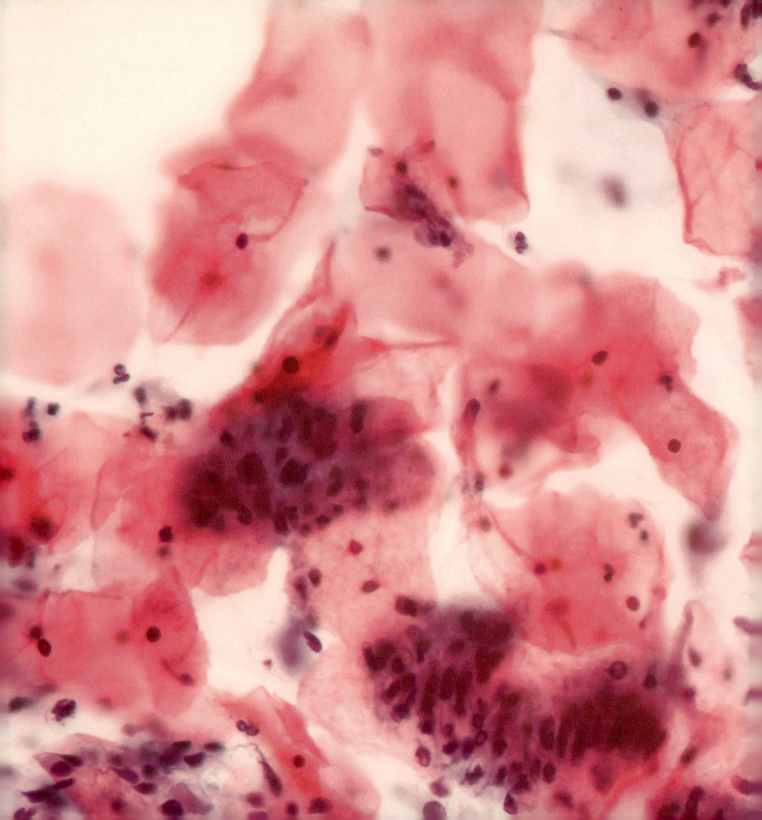

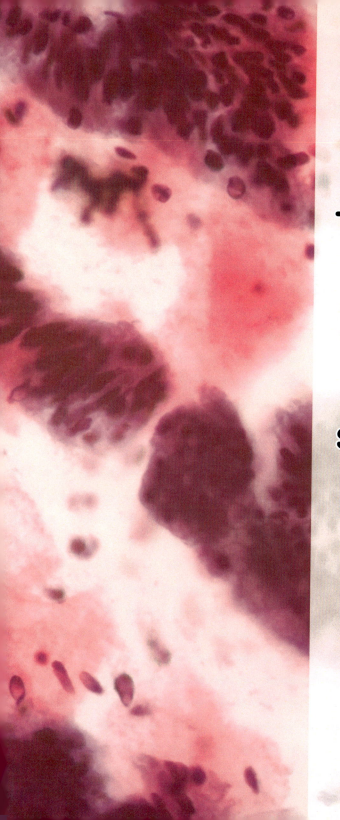

The glandular cells function primarily for the production of complex substances. These include hormones and enzymes the body needs.

For example, the cells in the pancreas produce insulin, some cells in the breasts produce milk, and the cells in the mouth produce saliva.

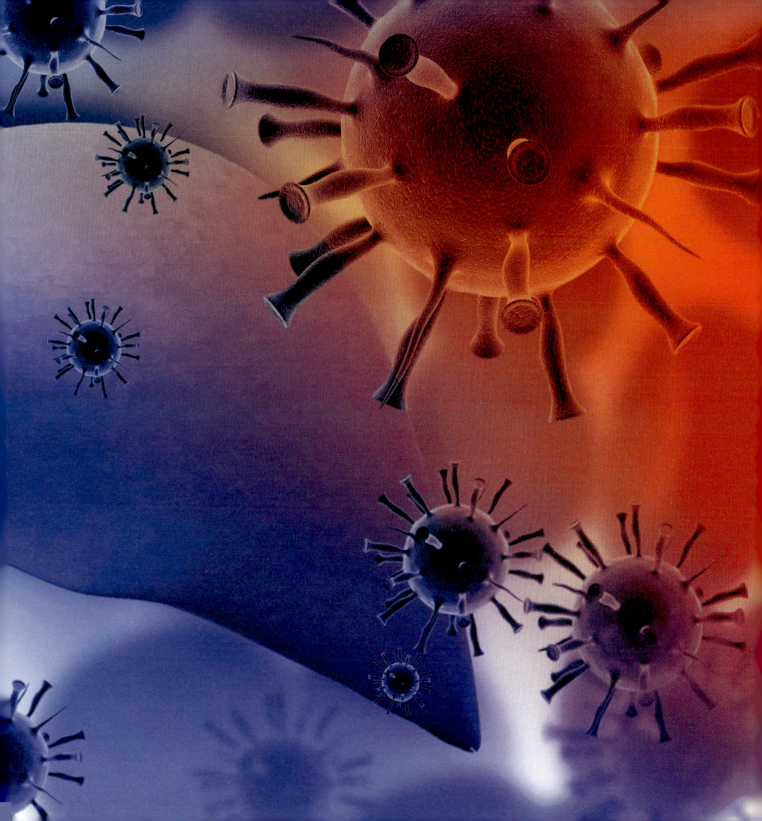

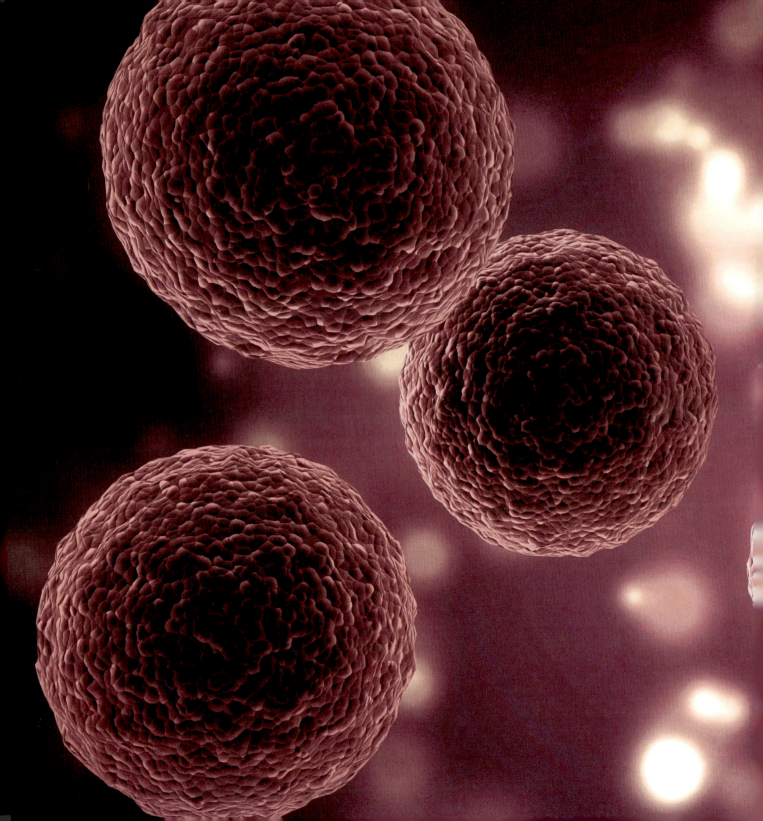

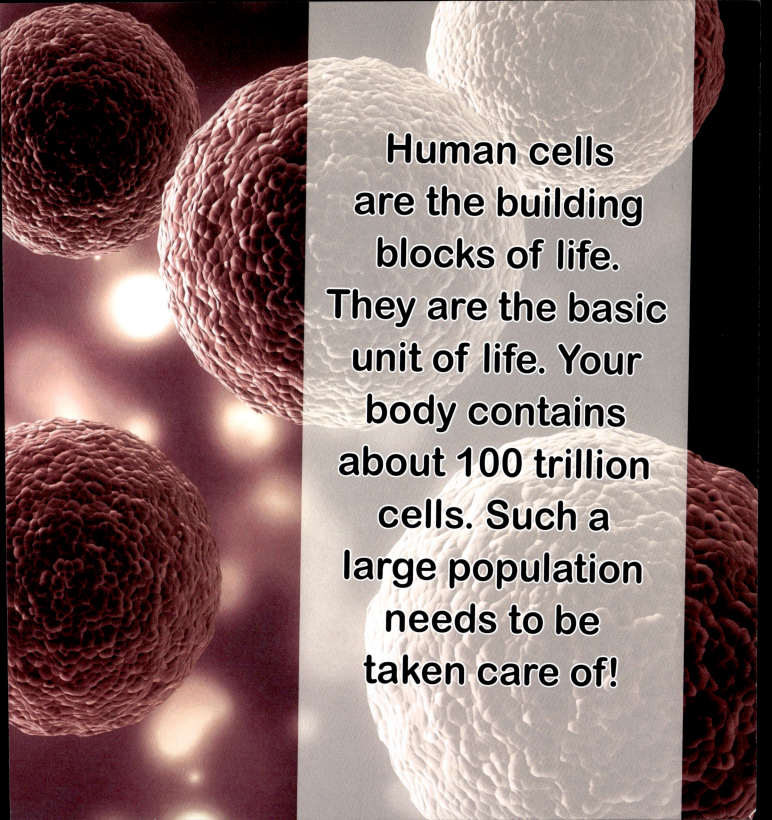

Human cells are the building blocks of life. They are the basic unit of life. Your body contains about 100 trillion cells. Such a large population needs to be taken care of!

There is much
more to learn
about our
human cells.
Research and
have fun!

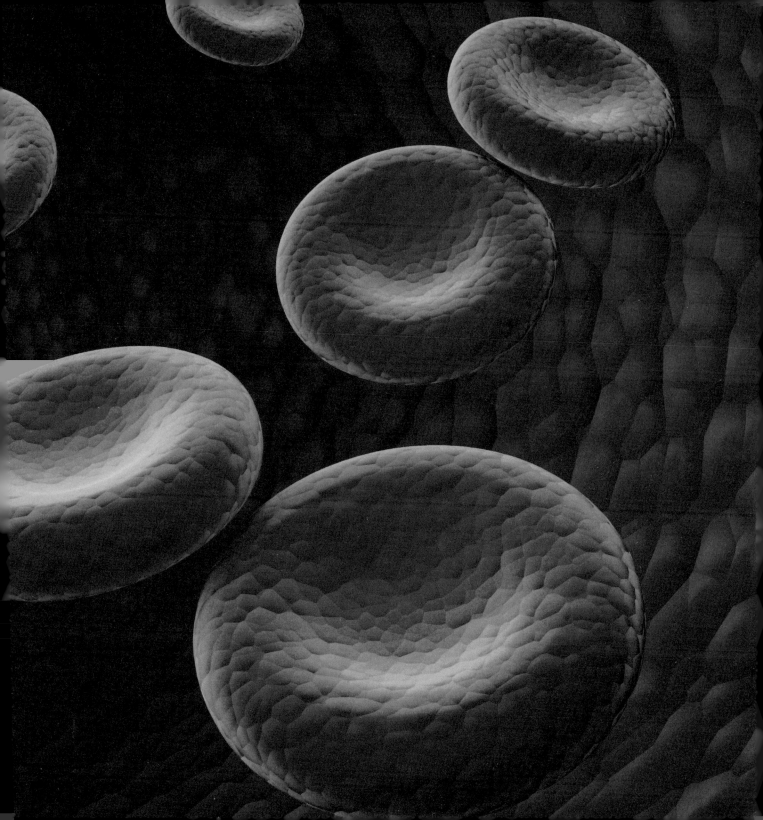

Made in the USA
Middletown, DE
26 February 2018